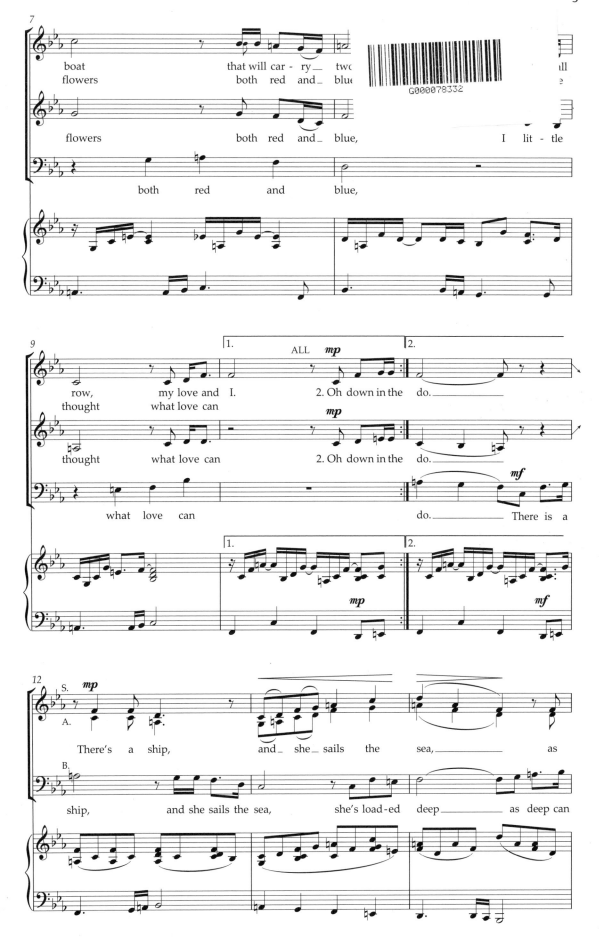

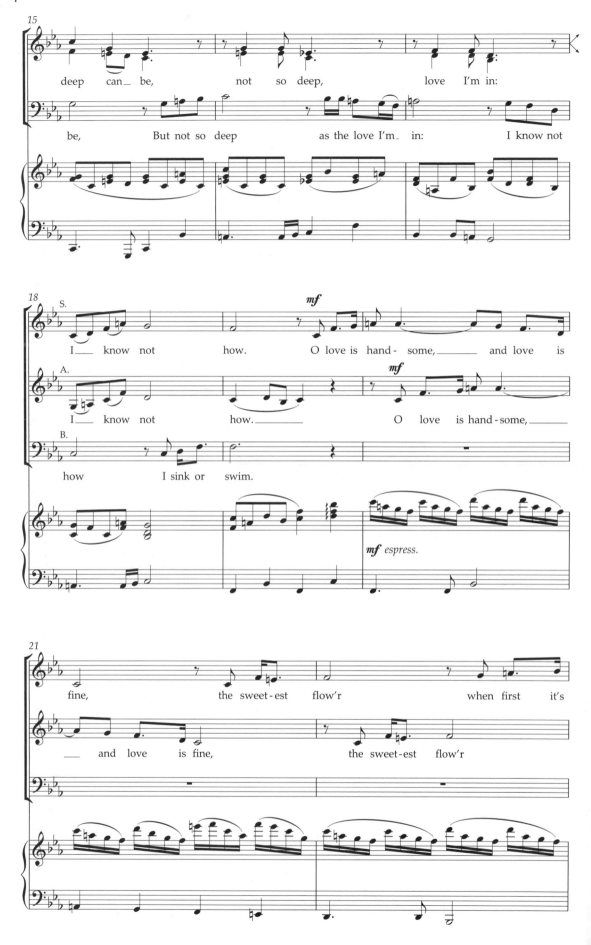

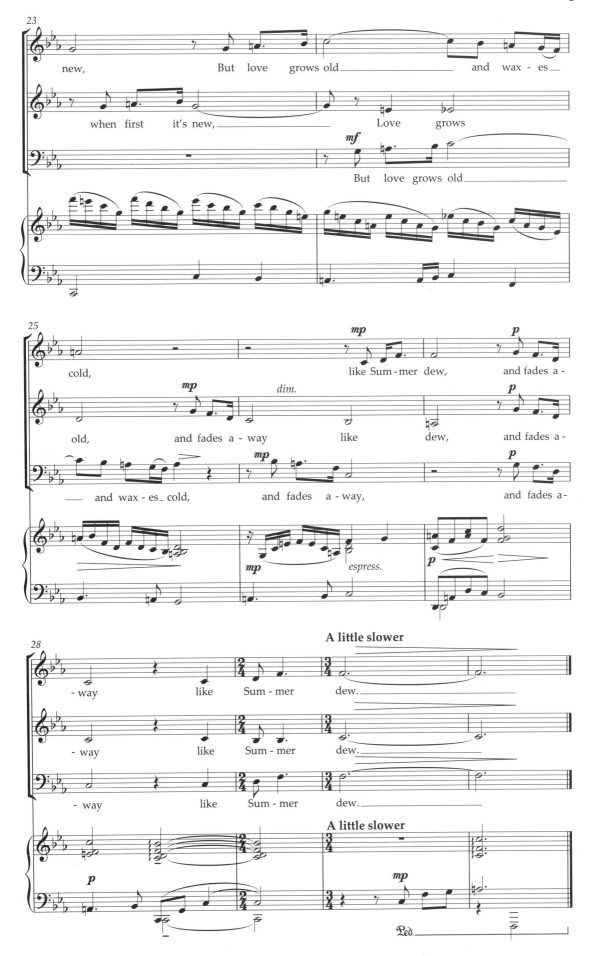

O waly waly

English traditional
arr. Alexander L'Estrange

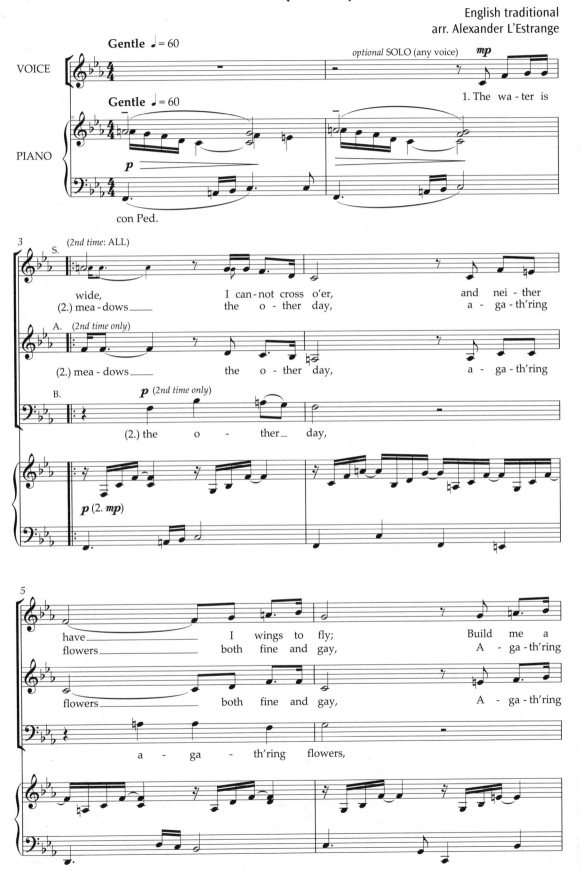

Voicing: **SAB and piano**

Faber Choral Singles

O waly waly

Words and Music: **English traditional**

Arranged by **Alexander L'Estrange**

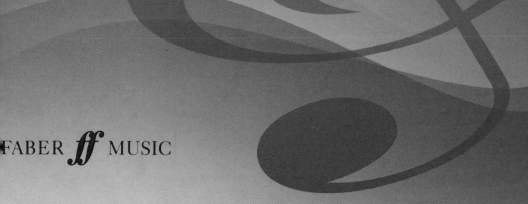

Faber ff MUSIC